# Hipster STREET LIFE Coloring Book

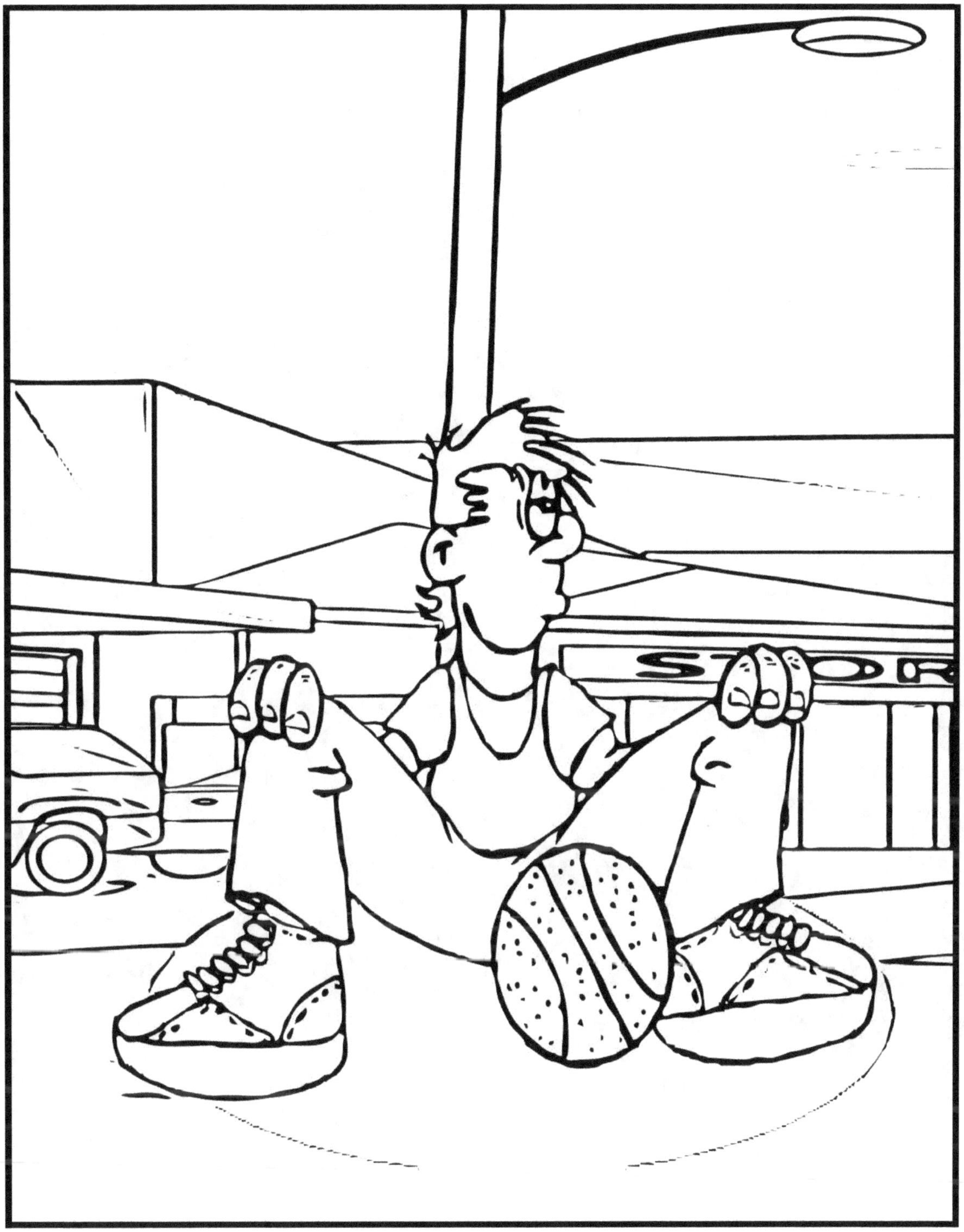
STOR

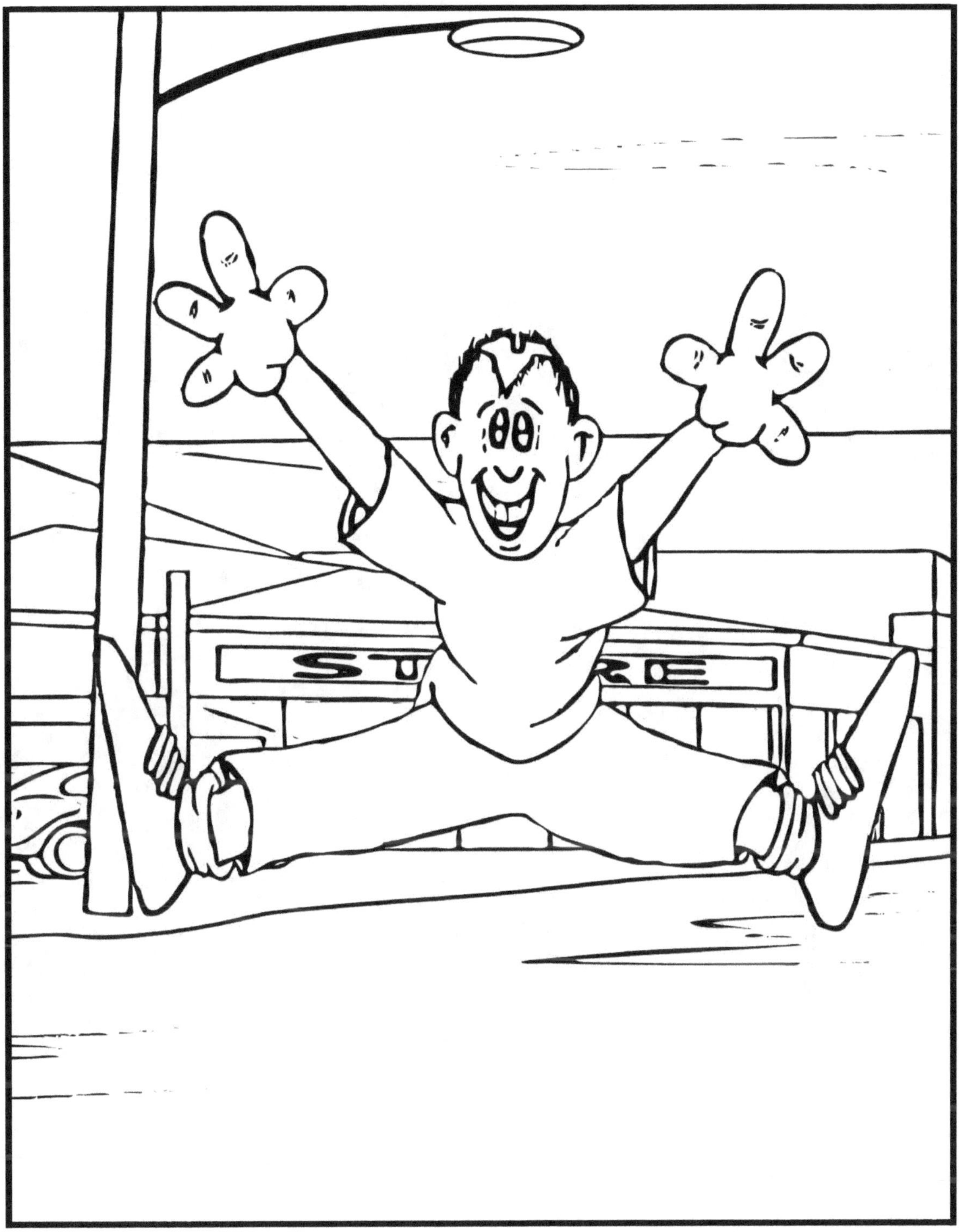

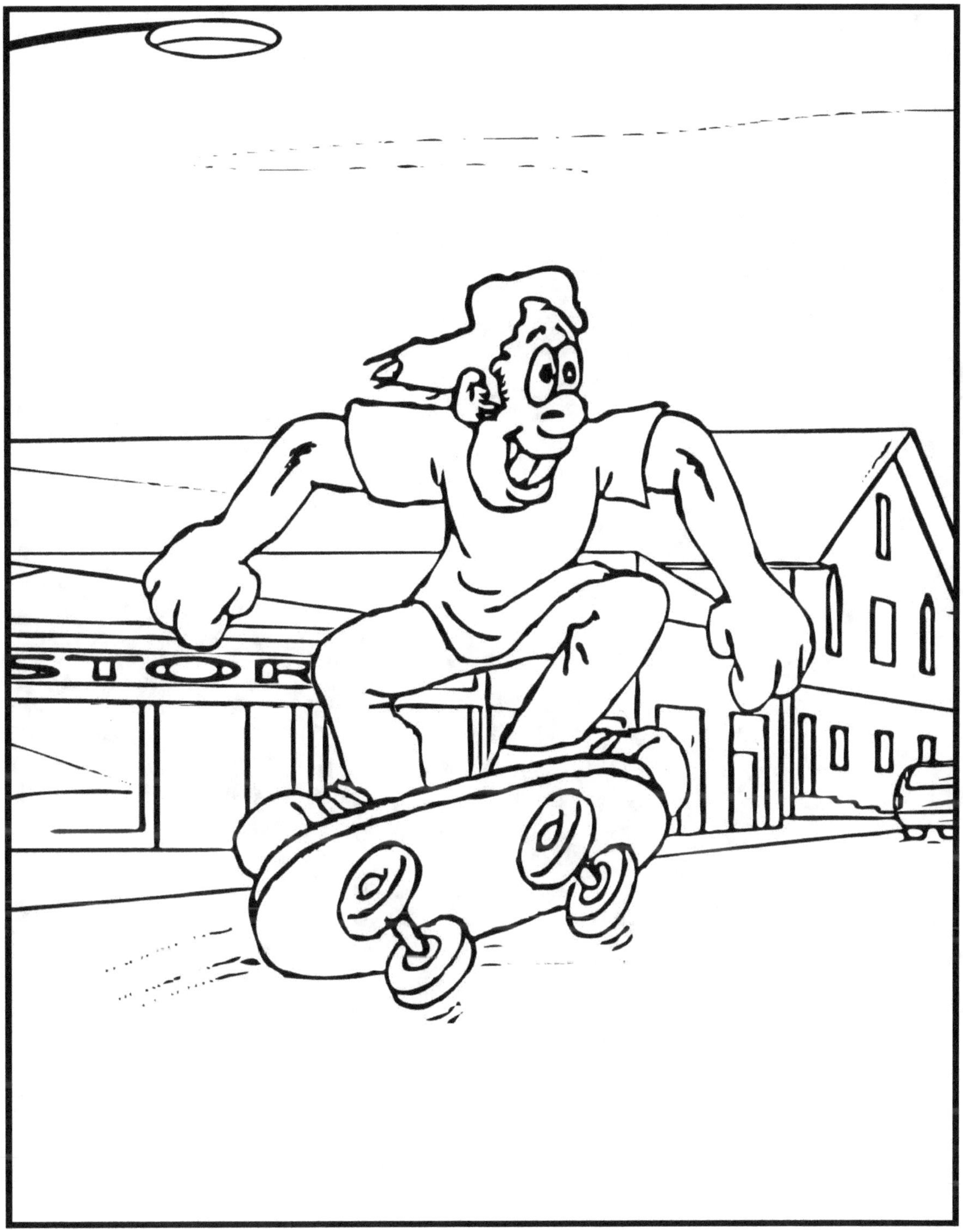
STOR

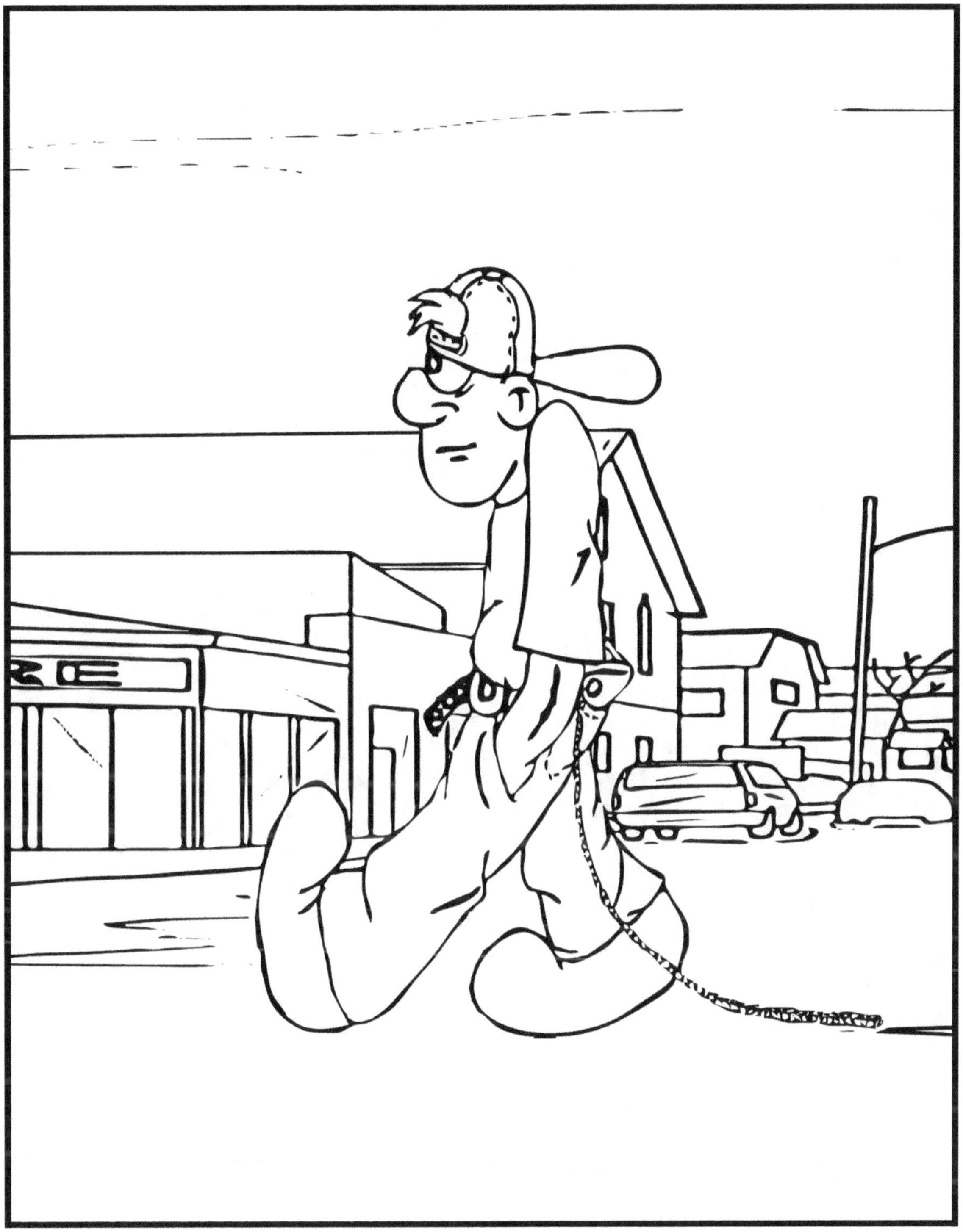
RE

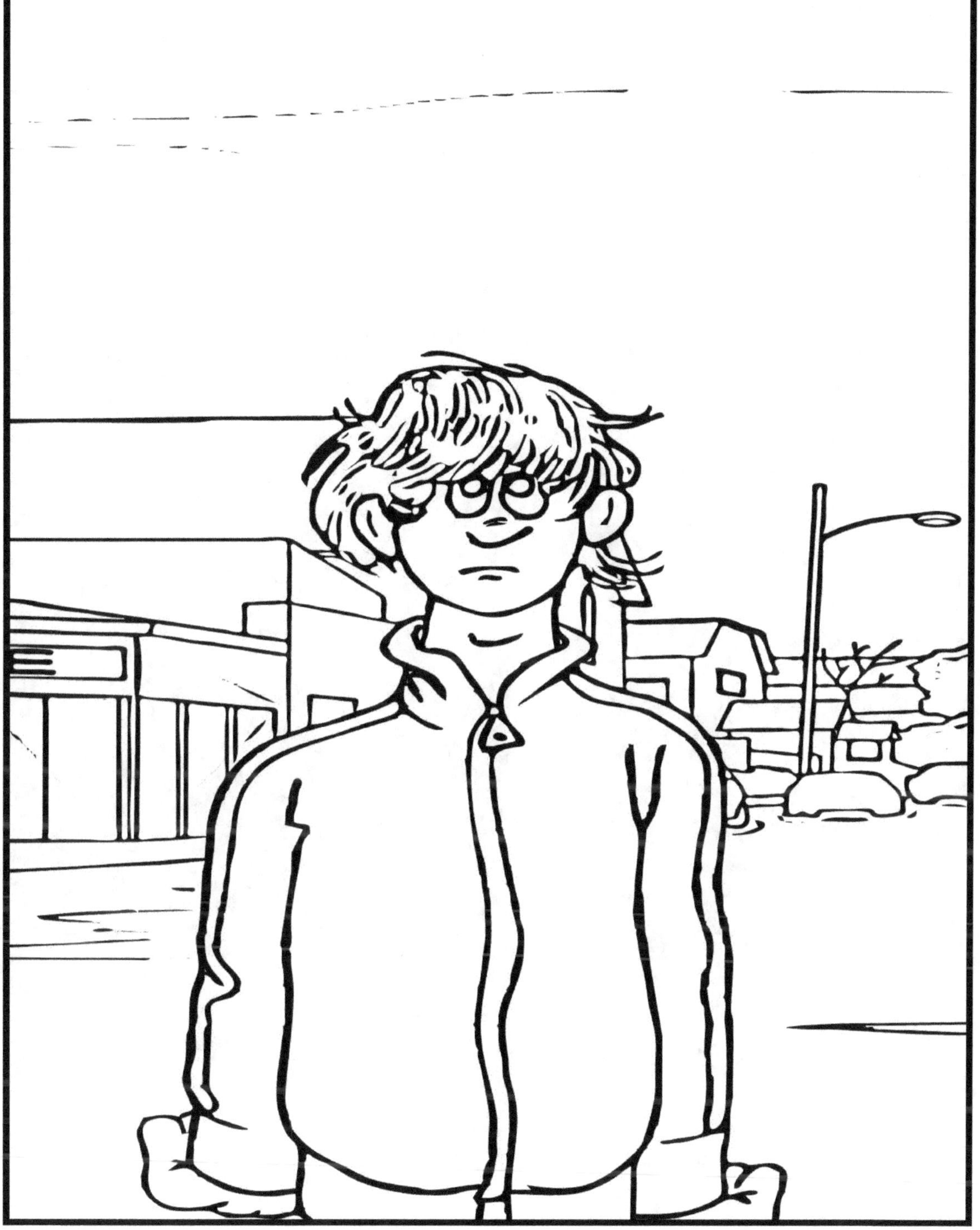

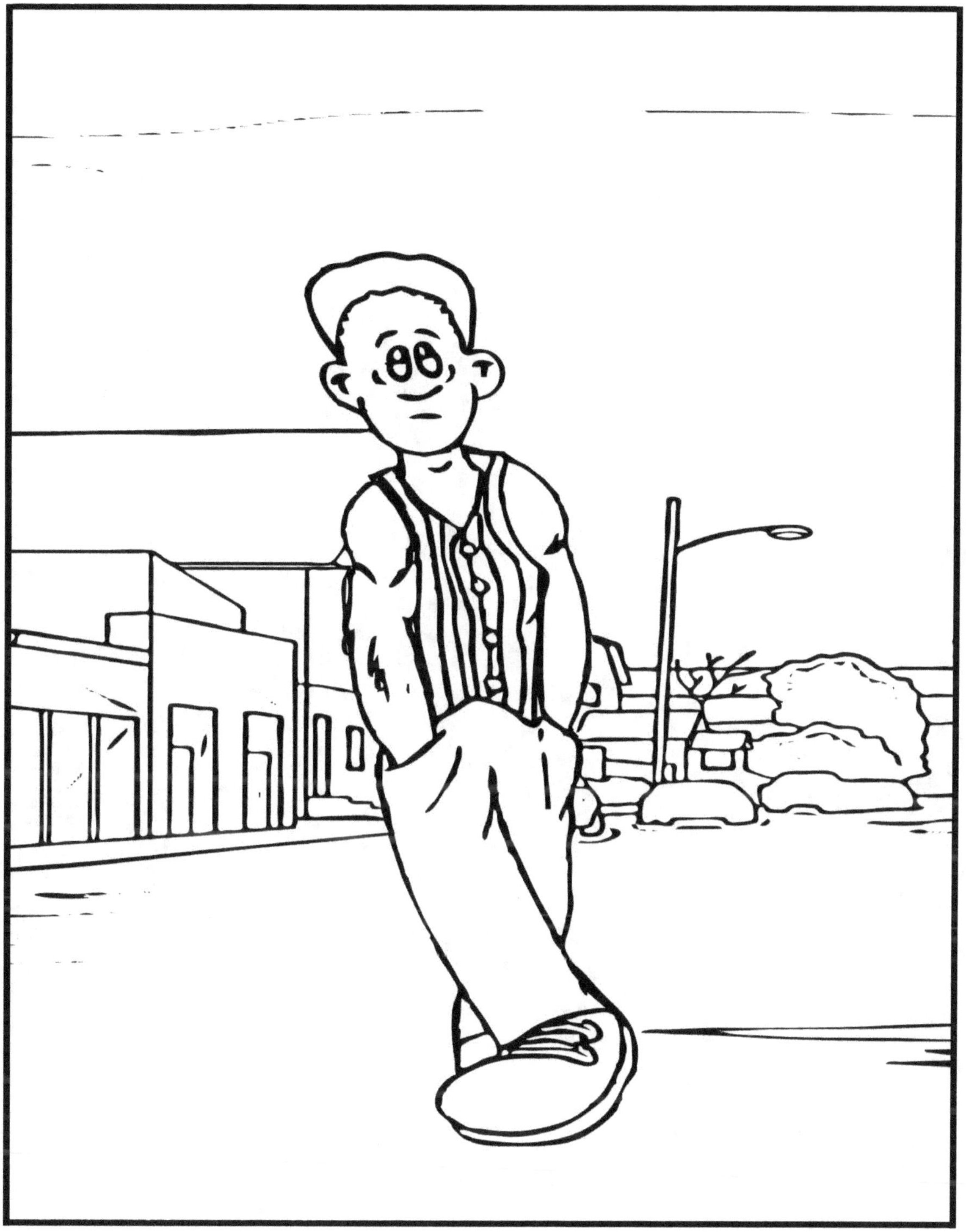

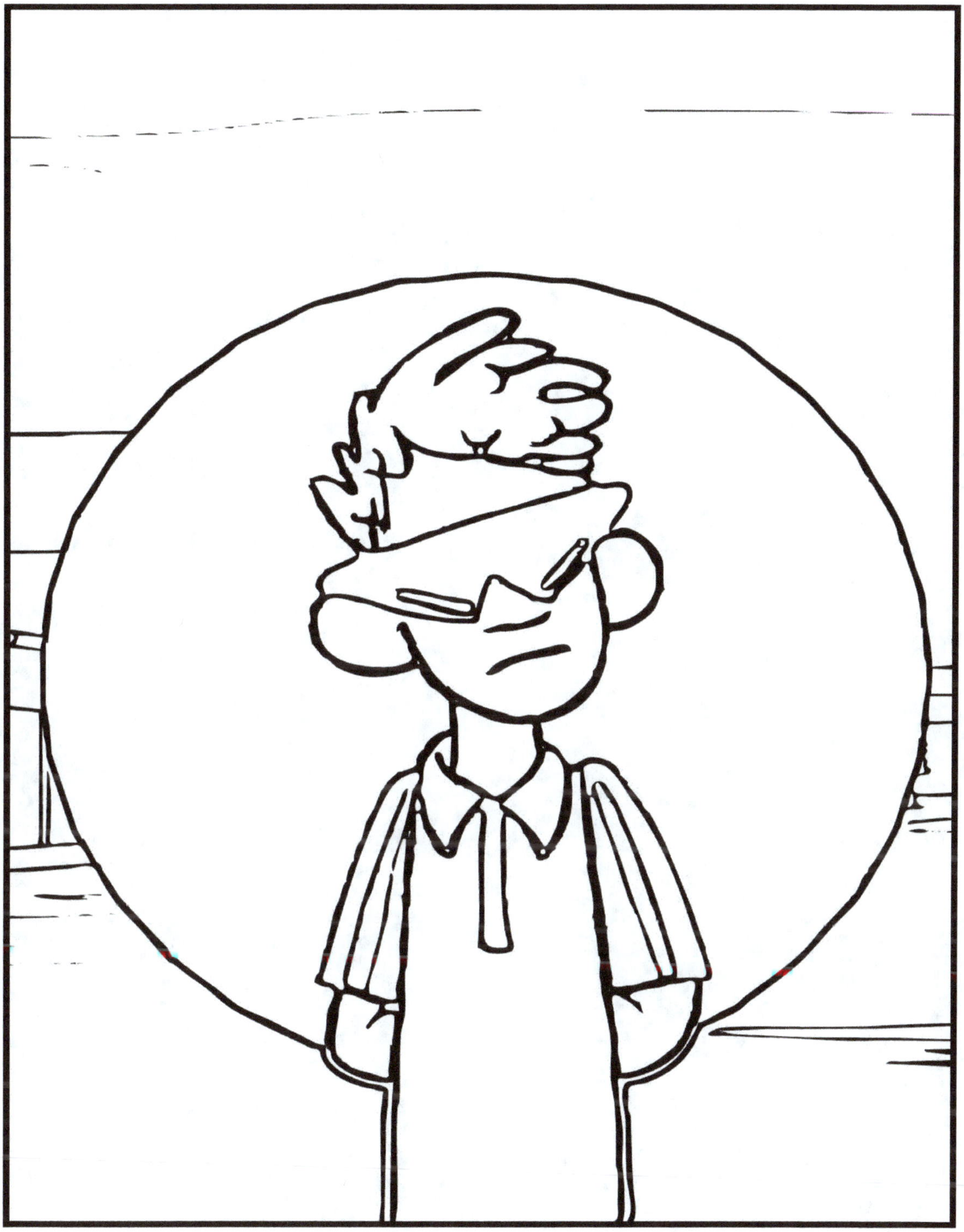

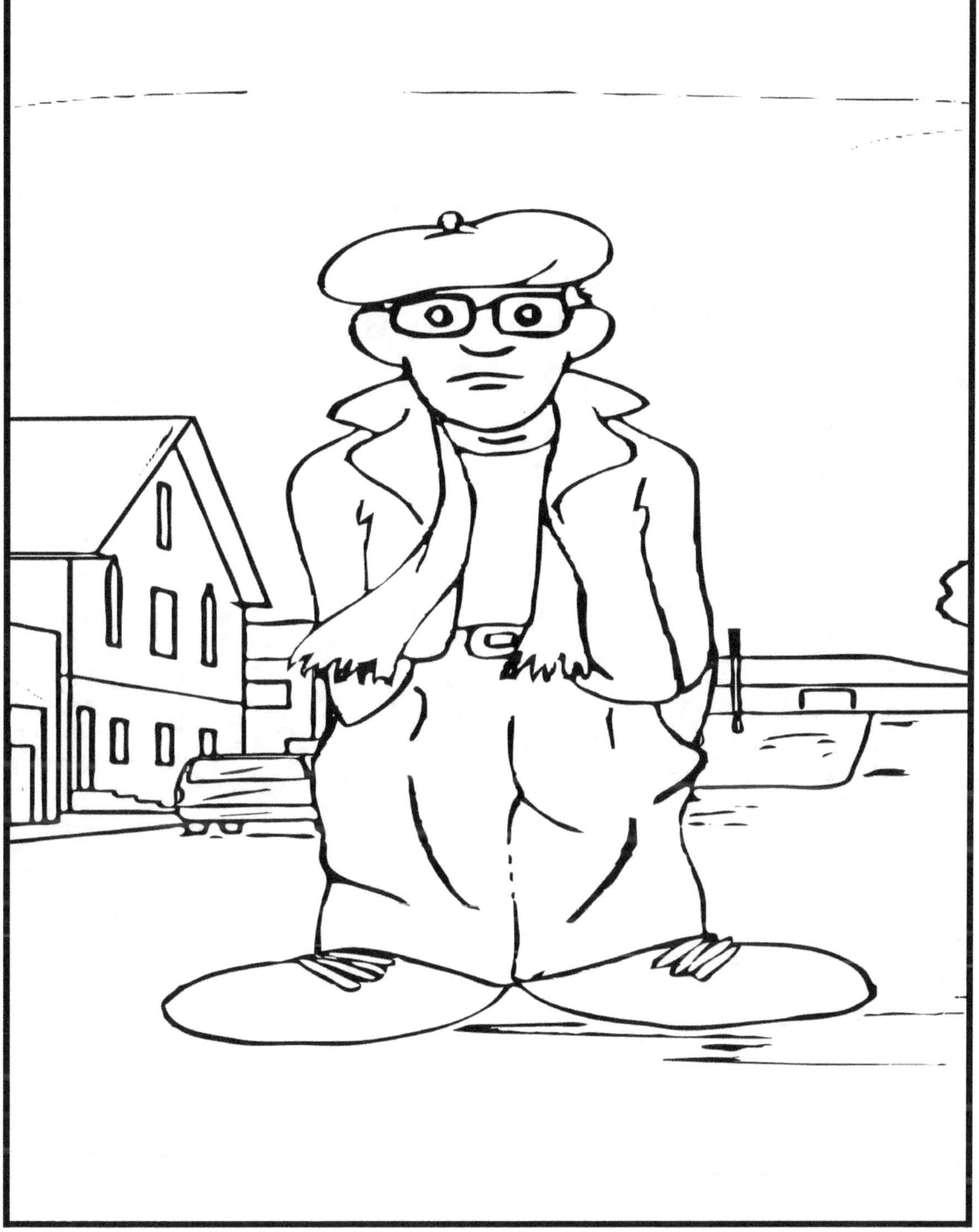

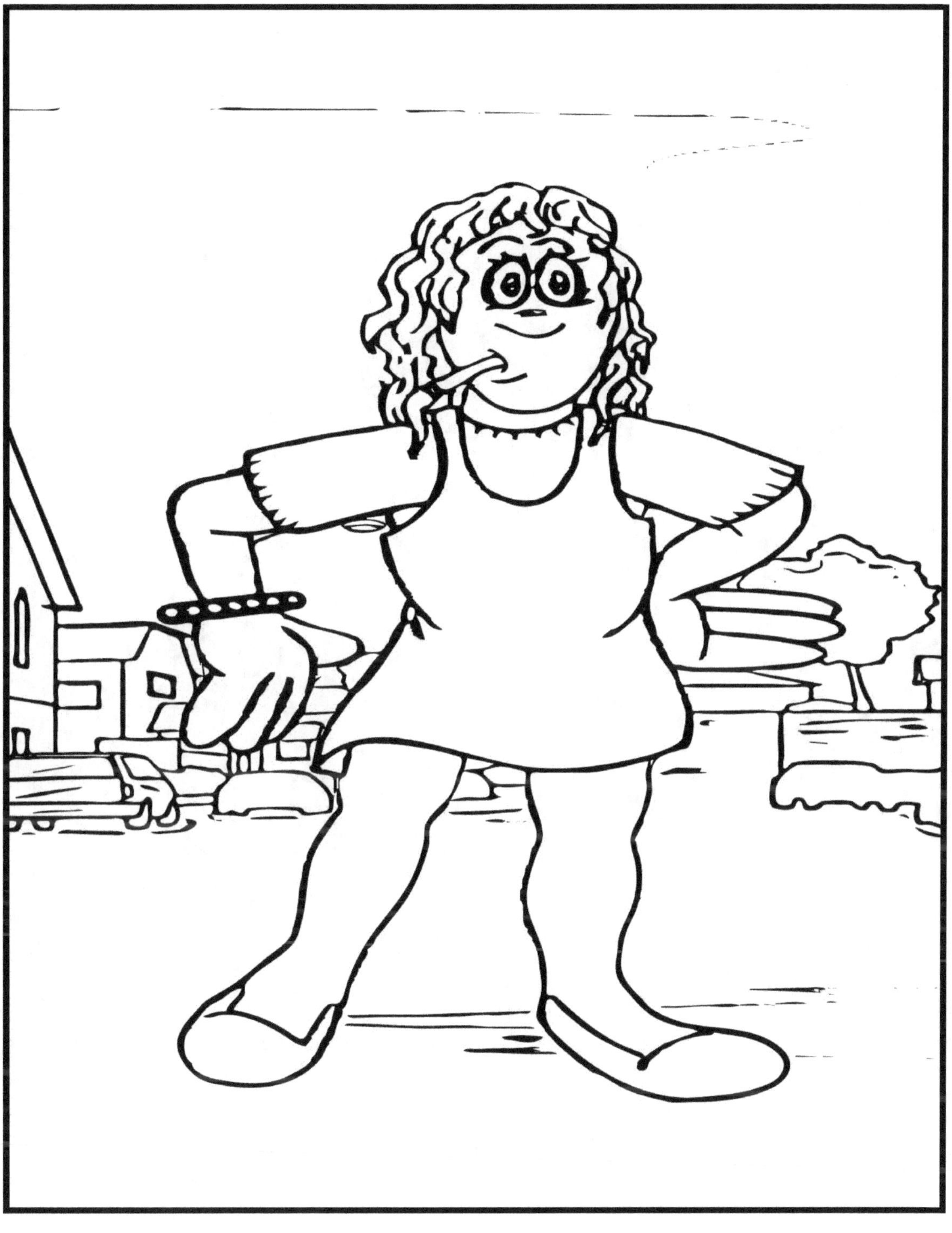

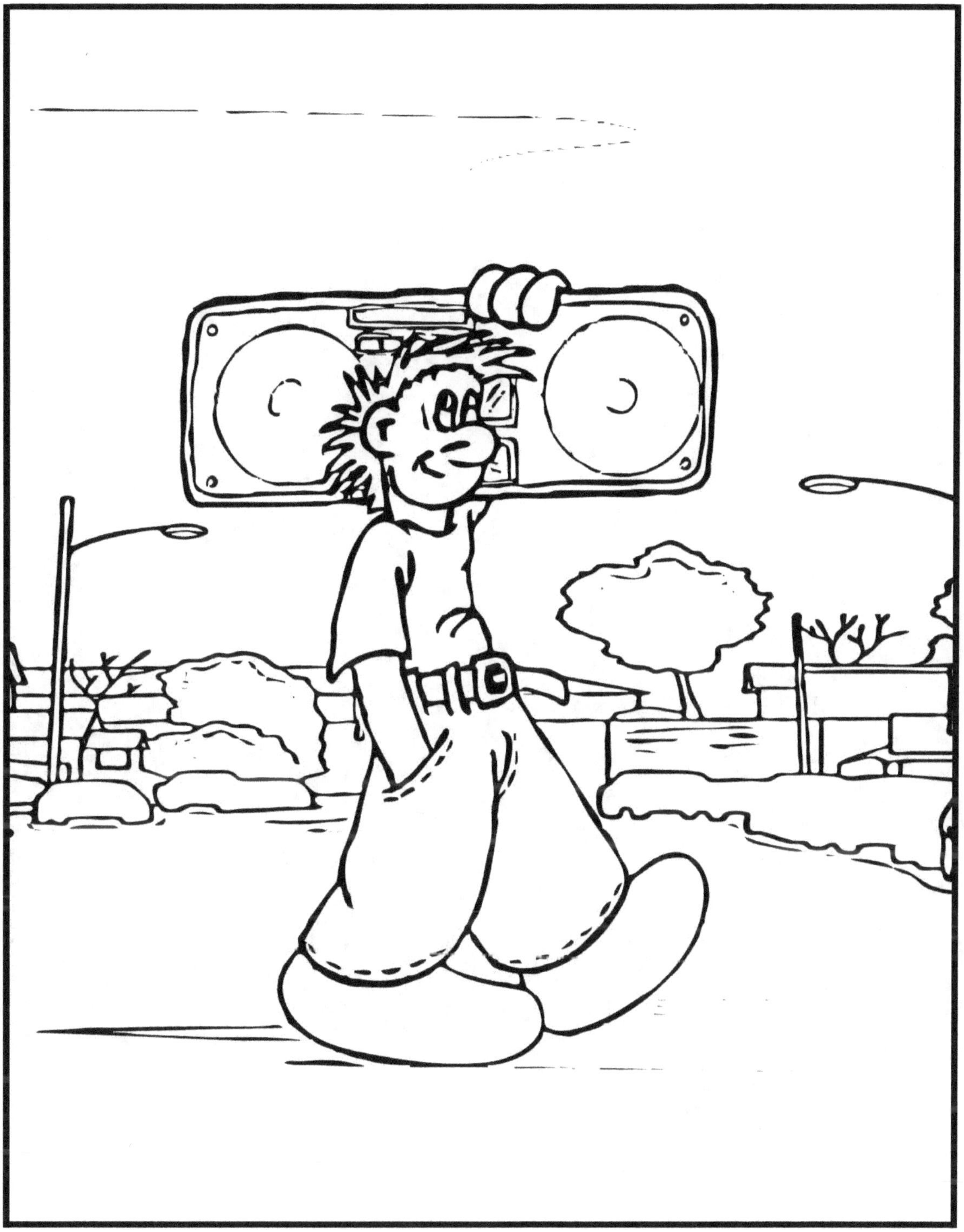

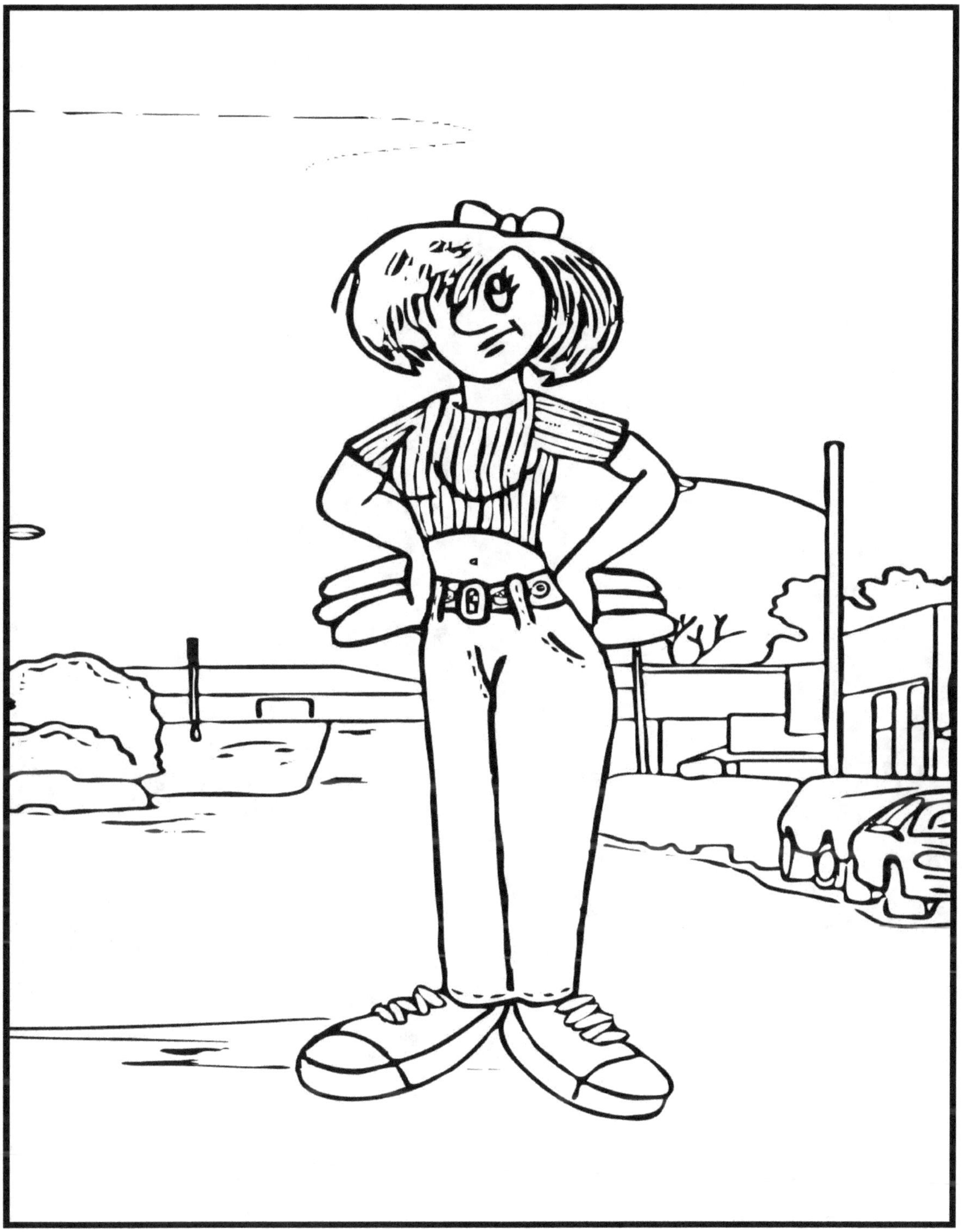

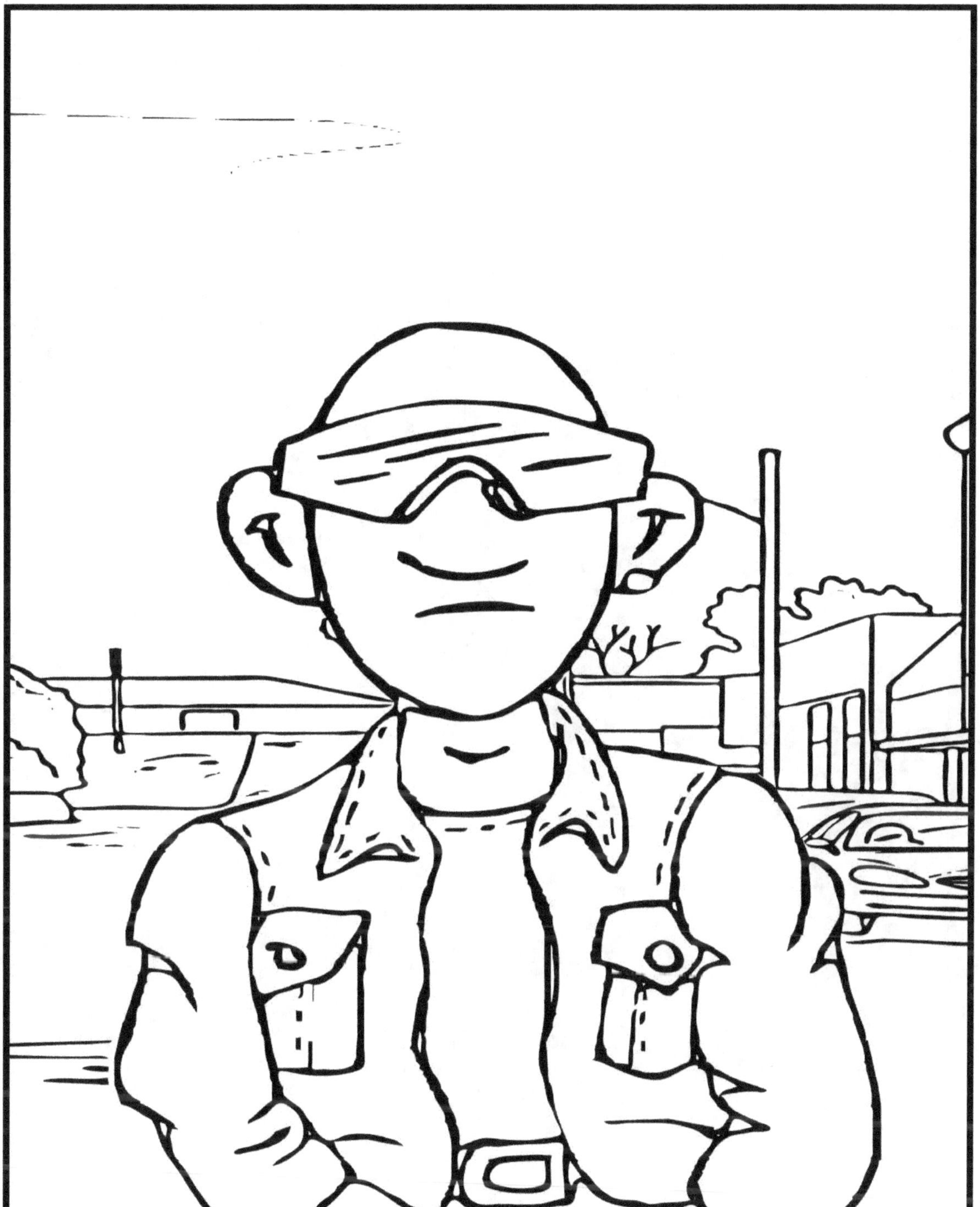

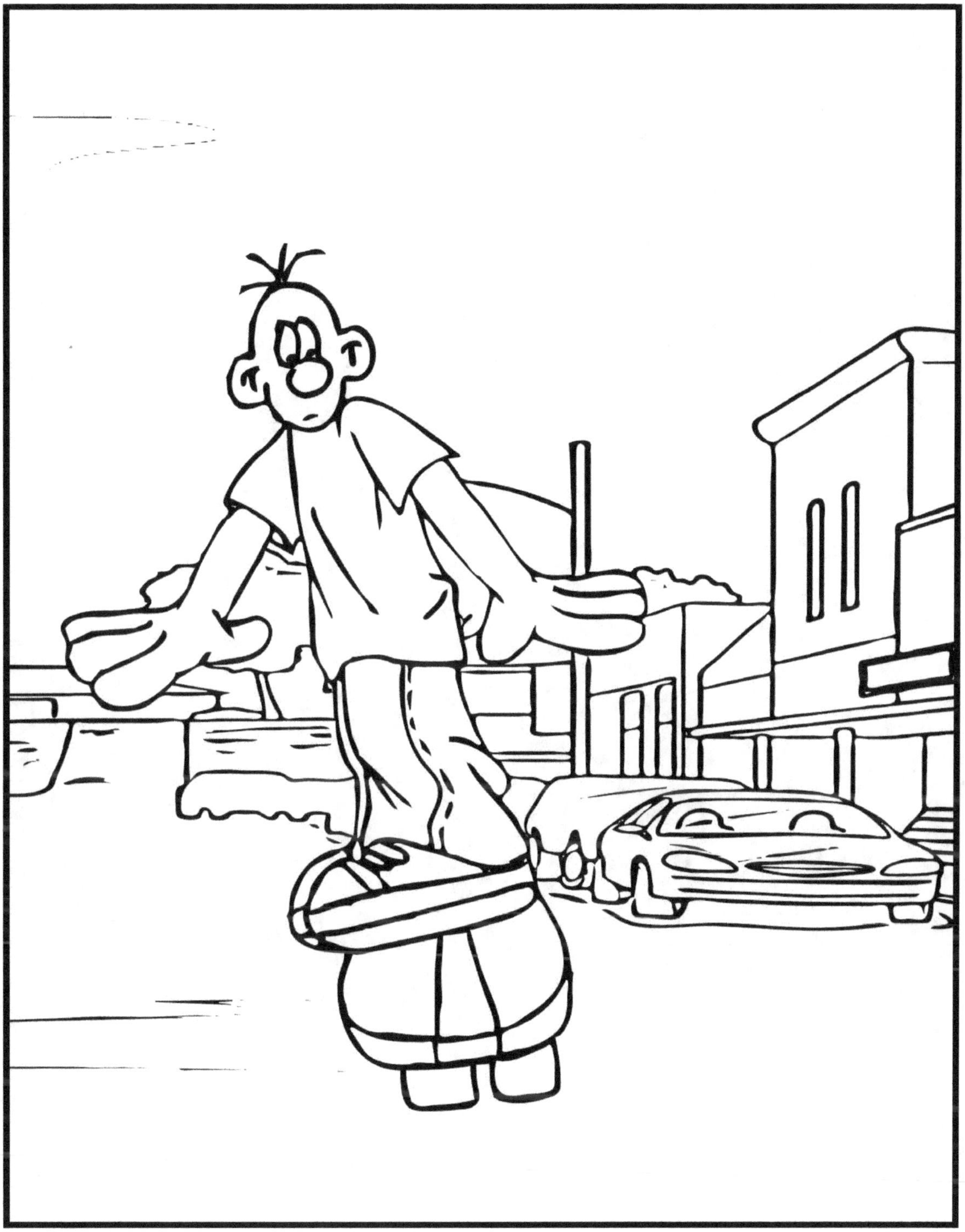

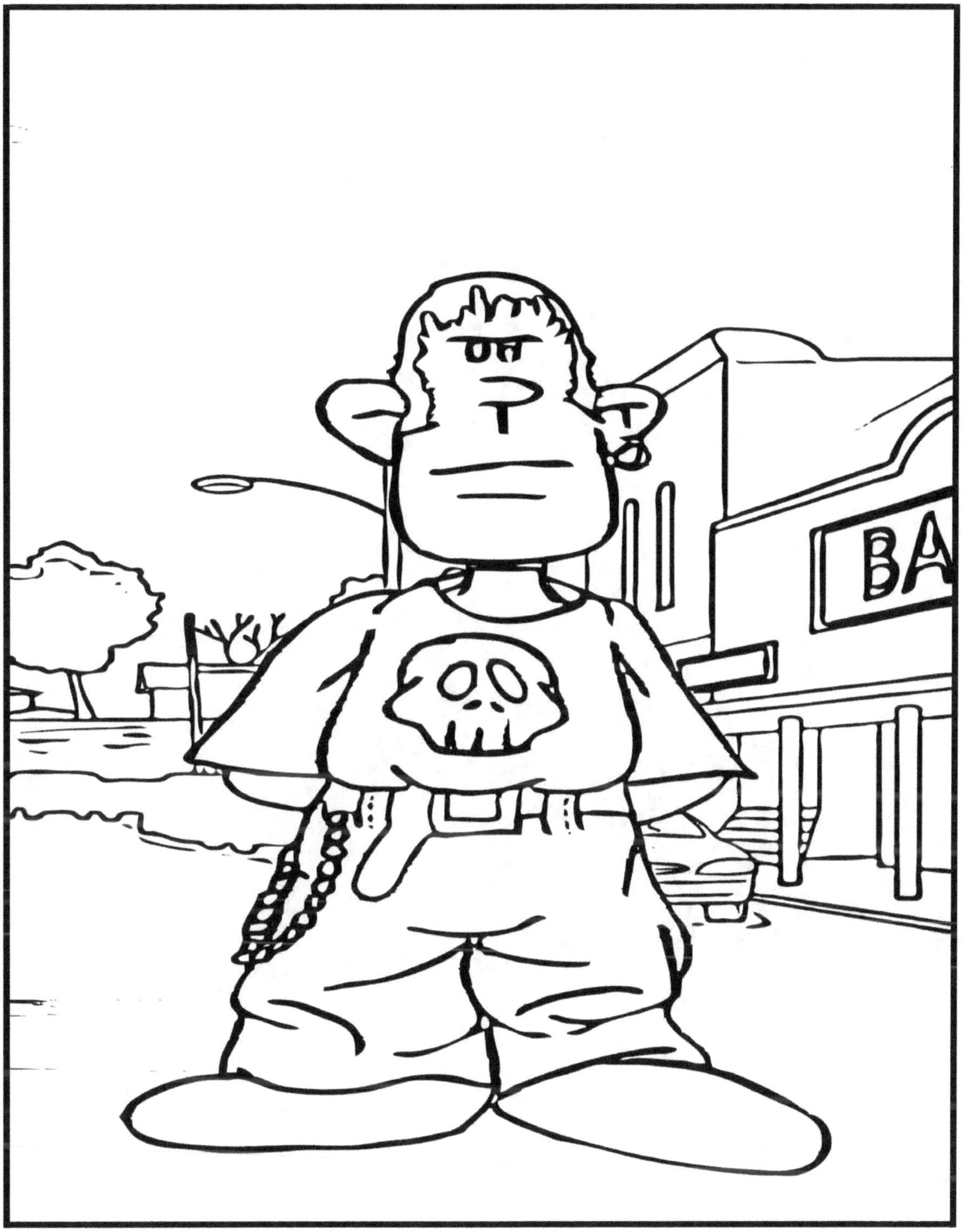
BA

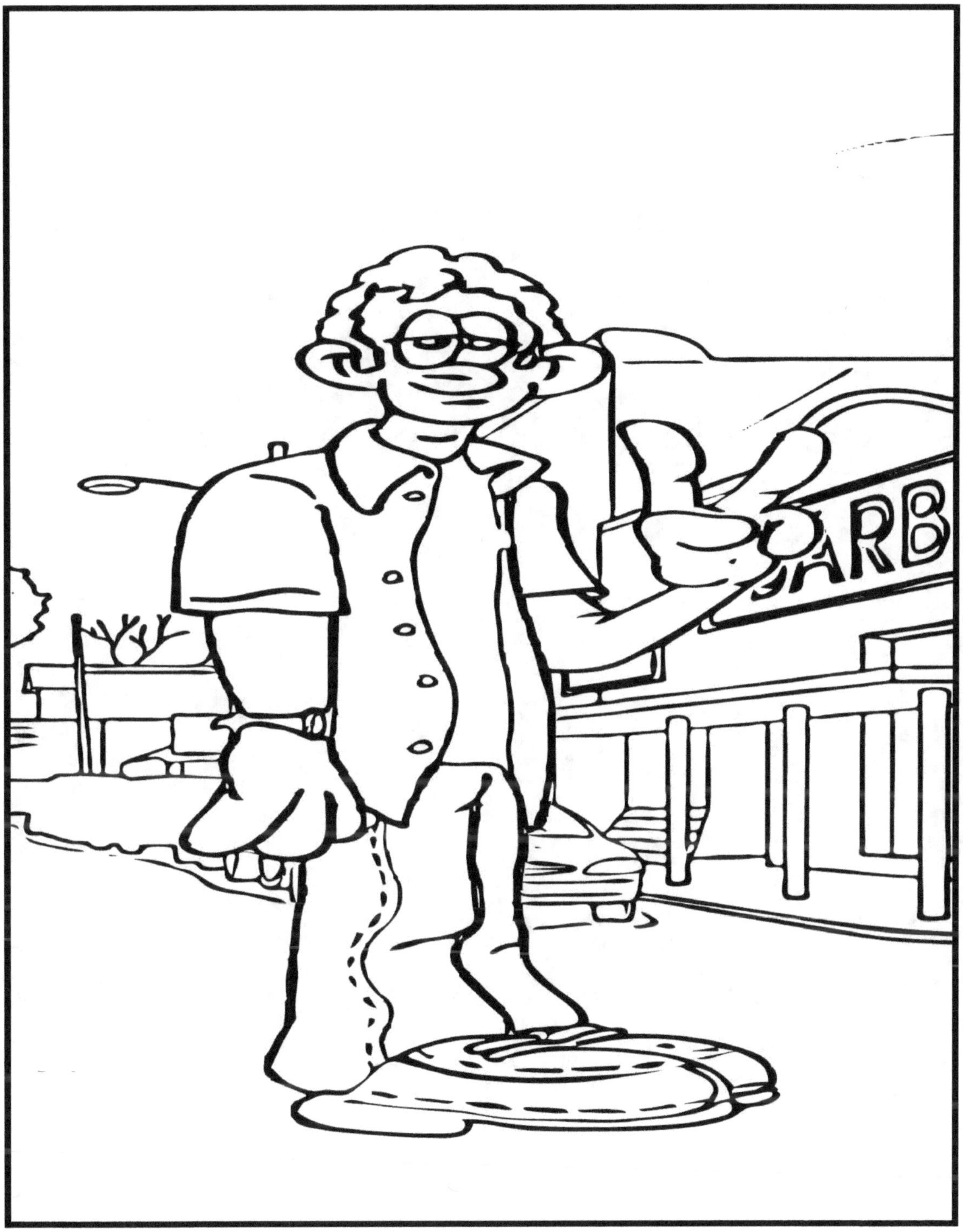

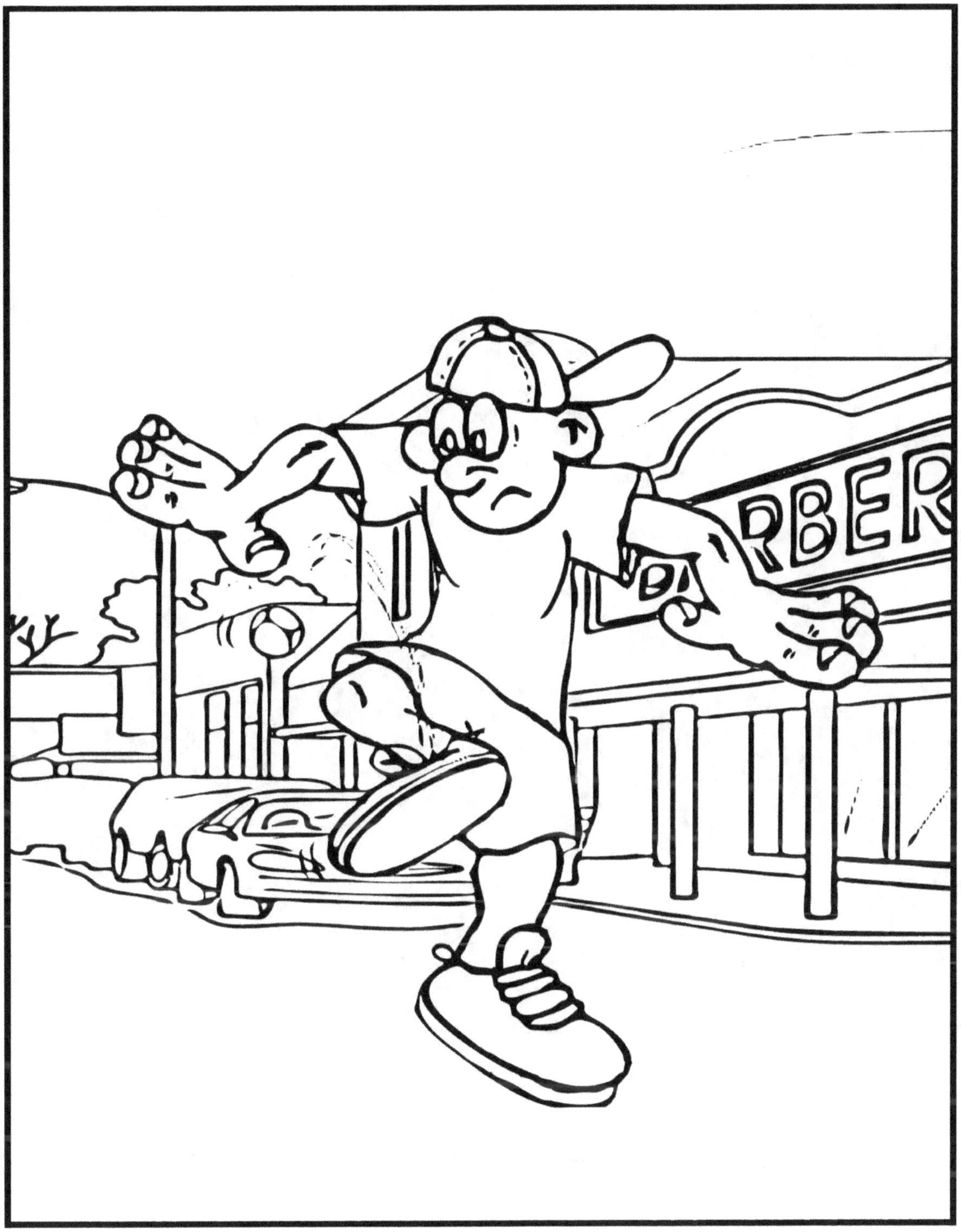
RBER

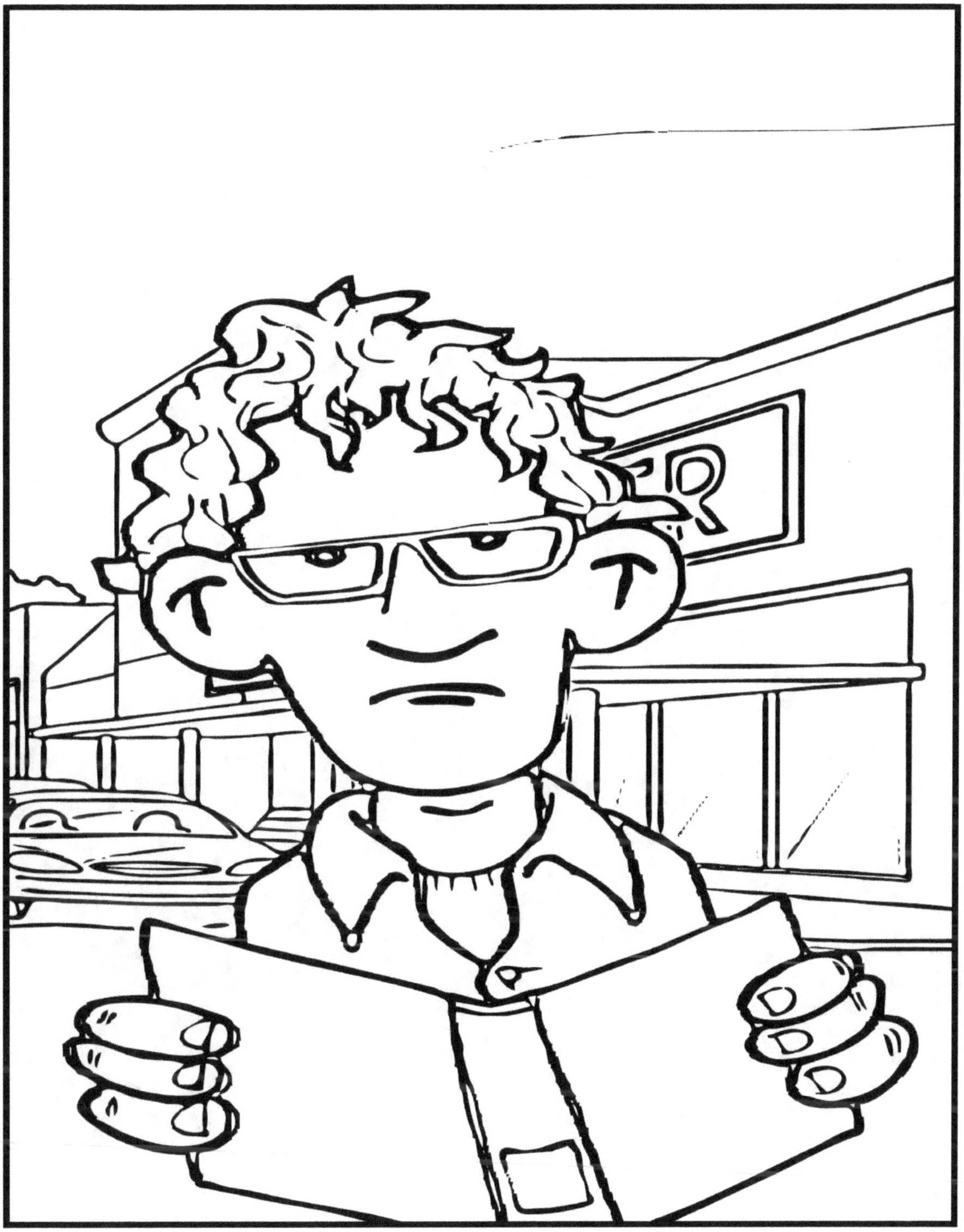

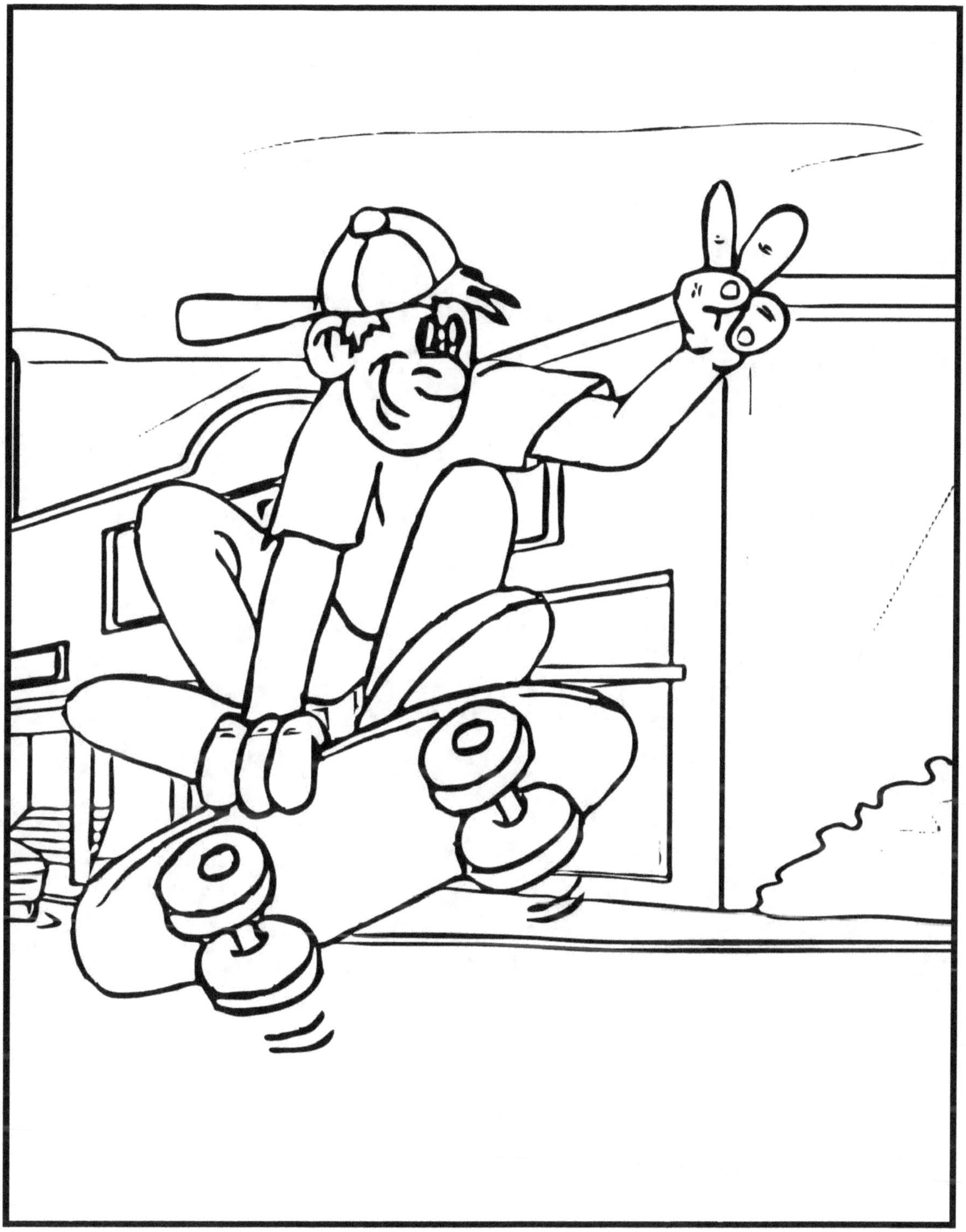

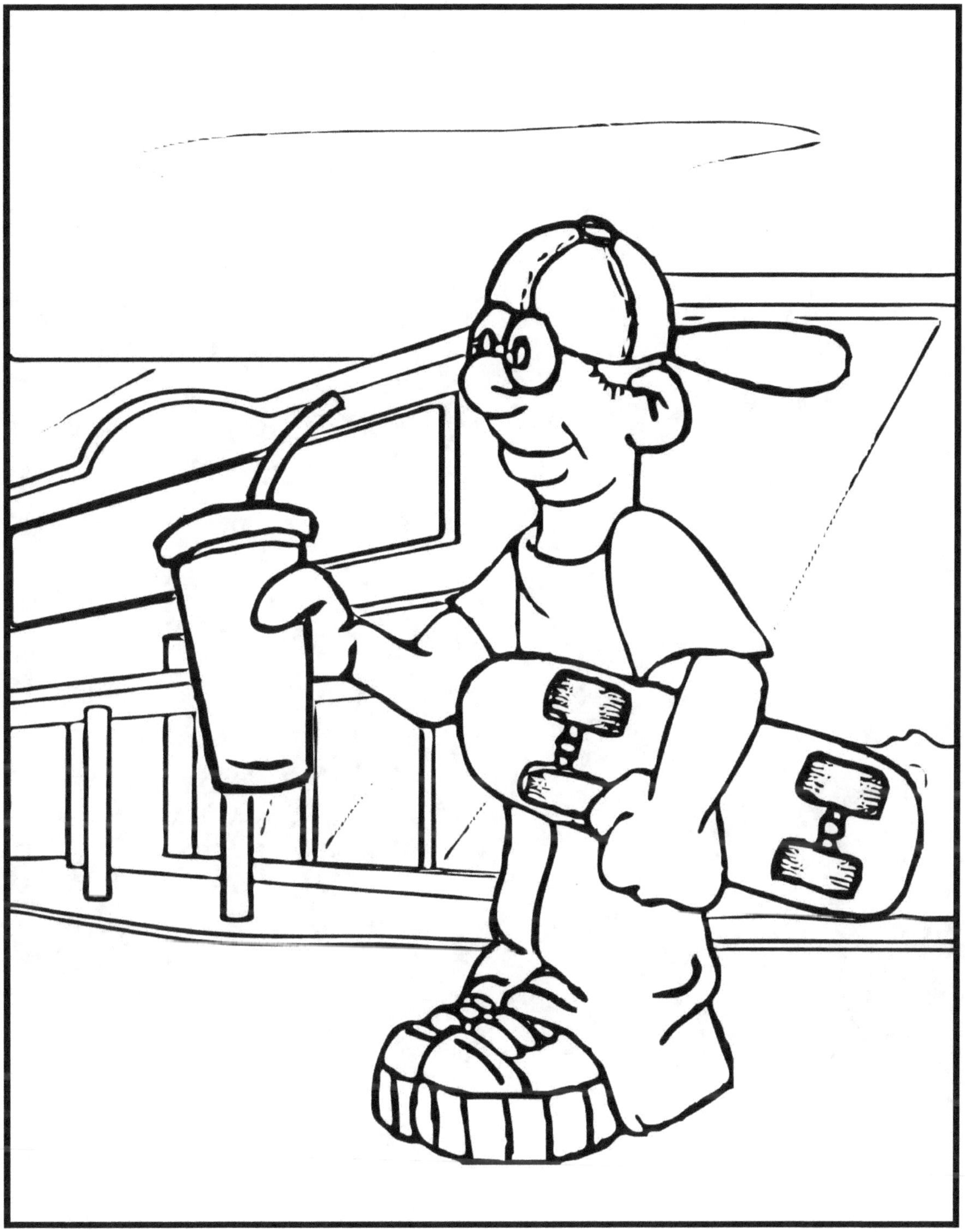

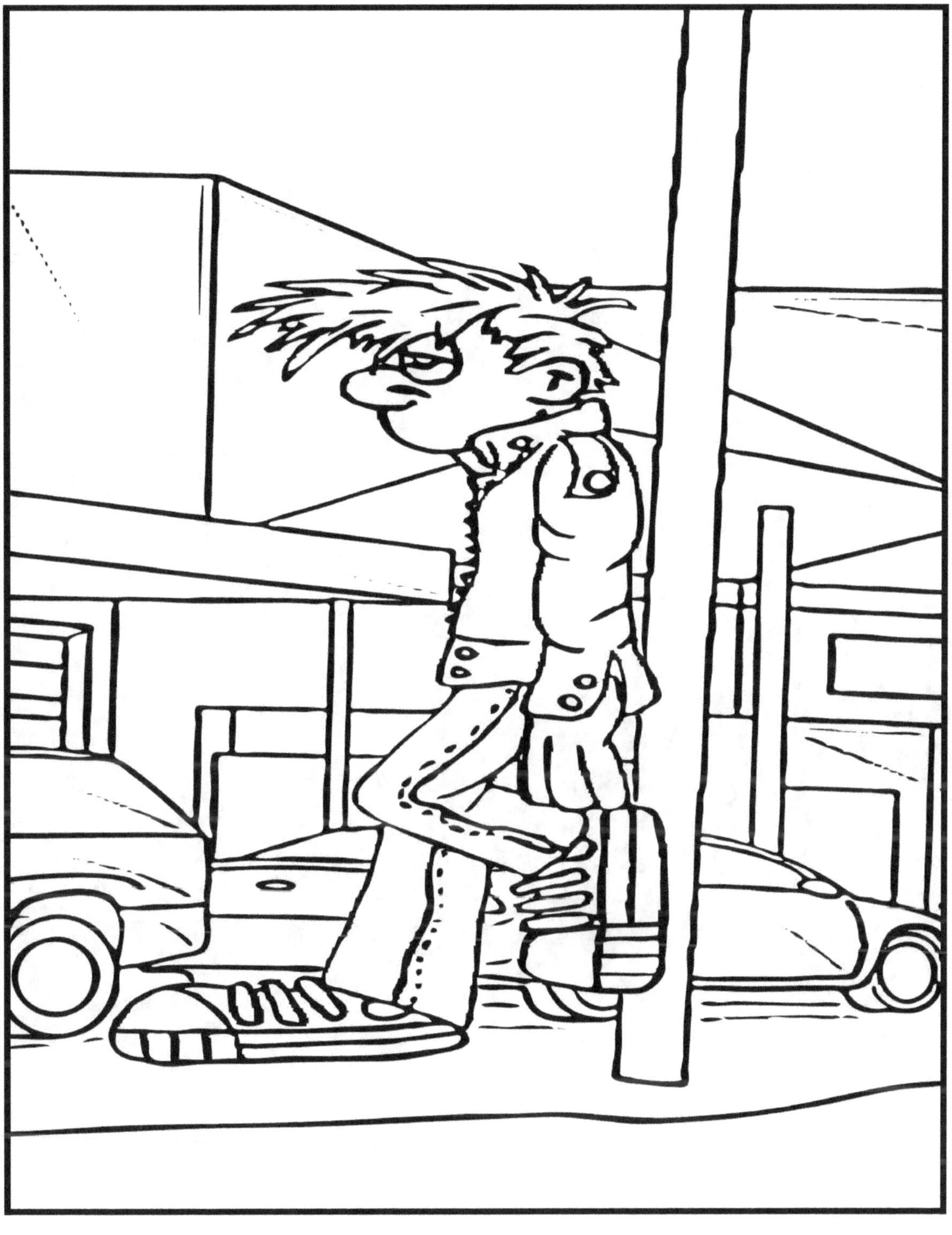

www.ingramcontent.com/pod-product-compliance
Lightning Source LLC
Chambersburg PA
CBHW081401170526
45166CB00010B/3166